PUERTO RICO

PUERTO RICO

Zachery Winslow

CHELSEA HOUSE

LV3-005086

Library of Congress Cataloging-in-Publication Data

Winslow, Zachery.
  Puerto Rico.
  Includes index.
  Summary: Surveys the history, topography, people, and culture
of Puerto Rico, with an emphasis on the current economy, industry,
and place in the political world.

1. Puerto Rico.   [1. Puerto Rico]
I. Title.   II. Series.
FI958.3.W56   1986   972.95   86-11688

ISBN 1-55546-154-9

Editorial Director: Susan R. Williams
Senior Editor: Rebecca Stefoff
Associate Editor:Rafaela Ellis
Art Director: Maureen McCafferty
Series Designer: Anita Noble
Project Coordinator: Kathleen P. Luczak

ACKNOWLEDGEMENTS

The author and publishers are grateful to these organizations for information and
photographs: American Petroleum Institute; National Air and Space Administration;
National Baseball Library; Puerto Rico Federal Affairs Administration; Puerto Rico
Tourism Company. Picture research: Imagefinders, Inc.

Contents

N

NORTH ATLANTIC OCEAN

Arecibo

Aguadilla

Río

Grande de Arecibo

Mayaguez

Cordillera Central

PUERTO

Ponce

Phosphorescent Bay

UNITED STATES

ATLANTIC OCEAN

GULF OF MEXICO

BAHAMAS

PUERTO RICO

HAITI

MEXICO

CUBA

DOMINICAN
REPUBLIC

BELIZE

JAMAICA

HONDURAS

GUATEMALA

NICARAGUA

EL SALVADOR

PANAMA

COSTA RICA

Map: Carol Molyneaux

San Juan

International Airport

△ *El Yunque*

CULEBRA

Caguas

Sierra de Luquillo

VIEQUES

ICO

Guayama

CARIBBEAN SEA

El Morro fortress was built to protect Puerto Rico from attack

The Rich Port

The Commonwealth of Puerto Rico is a lovely, lush island about 1,000 miles (1,600 kilometers) off the coast of southeastern Florida. The island is filled with craggy mountains and deep valleys. The waters surrounding it are some of the deepest in the entire Atlantic Ocean. For years, Puerto Rico has been a tourist attraction for many mainland Americans. Its year-round mild climate, its many white, sandy beaches, and its extraordinary hotels make this Caribbean island a favored vacation spot. It is administered by the United States, although it is not a state.

Puerto Rico, Spanish for "rich port," was discovered by Christopher Columbus in 1493 and is believed to be the only place in the United States where Columbus actually landed. At the time of its discovery, the rectangle-shaped island was claimed for Spain, and its Spanish heritage has been preserved for centuries.

Many facets of life in Puerto Rico—its interesting history, its people, its bilingual Spanish-American culture, and its struggle between commonwealth and statehood status—make it not only a vacation island but a remarkable place, full of festivity, cultural activity, and family life. Let's take a closer look at Puerto Rico, the rich port of the Caribbean.

The rolling hills of Puerto Rico are thick with vegetation

The Land

Perhaps the best way to explore and understand a foreign land, other than to visit it, is to study its geography—the mountains, rivers, vegetation, and wildlife that make a place unique.

The island of Puerto Rico is about 100 miles (160 kilometers) long from east to west, and about 35 miles (55 kilometers) from north to south. Including the major neighboring islands of Vieques (Crab Island), Culebra, and Mona, the total area of Puerto Rico is 3,435 square miles (8,897 square kilometers).

Puerto Rico is made up of four main land regions: the coastal lowlands, the coastal valleys, the foothills, and the central mountains. The first of these areas, the coastal lowlands, is actually two regions, which form the north and south coasts of the island. The northern lowlands cover an area as broad as eight to twelve miles (13 to 19 kilometers) and have a humid climate. Although the southern lowlands cover a narrower area and have, as a rule, a drier climate, sugar cane is an important crop in both areas. Puerto Rico's largest city and capital, San Juan, is located in the lowlands, as are the cities of Bayamon and Ponce.

Extending inland from both the east and west coasts of the island are the coastal valleys. Here, most of the land is used for growing sugar cane, coconuts, and other tropical fruits. One of the most serene fishing villages in Puerto Rico, Las Crobas, is found in a coastal valley.

Rising in two long, east-west chains, just inland from the coastal lowlands, are the foothills. They are filled with jagged peaks and deep basins formed when the limestone underlying them was washed away over many years, causing the slow erosion of the soil.

Cordillera Central is the major range in the region known as the central mountains. The range runs from east to west across the south-central part of the island and passes through the Toro Negro National Forest, about 50 miles from San Juan. Nestled in a valley of the Cordillera Central is the village of Villaba. The Cordillera Central also boasts the highest peak in Puerto Rico, the Cerra de Punta, which reaches 4,389 feet (1,338 meters). The northeastern section of the central mountains is called the Sierra de Luquillo. In the western part of the mountain region, coffee and citrus fruits are grown, while tobacco terraces are found in the mountain valleys and lower slopes.

Puerto Rico is a land not only of beaches but of rugged mountains and lush valleys; although agriculture is a major industry, soil erosion is a constant problem

Puerto Rico's coastline, filled with many harbors and beaches, makes it a popular vacation spot. Some of the most beautiful and frequently visited beaches are Dorado (on the Atlantic Coast, just about 25 miles or 40 kilometers west of San Juan), Luquillo (about an hour's drive north of San Juan), and San Juan's Condado Strip, where there are many modern hotels. Puerto

Rico's general coastline measures 311 miles (501 kilometers), but its tidal shoreline, which is made up of hundreds of tiny inlets and bays, is 700 miles (1,127 kilometers) long.

Although there are more than 1,000 small streams and about 45 rivers in Puerto Rico, they are shallow and unsuitable for passage in large boats. All of these streams and rivers, including the Arecibo, the longest river, flow northward from the mountain ranges into the Atlantic Ocean. And while there are no natural lakes in Puerto Rico, artificial lakes such as Yauco in the southwestern hills (which was created by a dam on the Yauco River) are water sources for irrigation, industry, and hydroelectric power. The island's major ports are Ponce in the south and San Juan in the north.

Puerto Rico's coastline is ideal for sailing and sunbathing

The rain forest at El Yunque is a wonderland of waterfalls, animal life, and tropical plants

Many visitors to Puerto Rico are fooled by the bright, sunny days, but it is not at all unusual for some rain to fall on the island every day, especially in the afternoon. Just like the neighboring island of St. Thomas in the U.S. Virgin Islands, Puerto Rico experiences brief but heavy rainfall. Many an energetic game of tennis on the hotel courts has been interrupted by these sudden downpours. In general, however, rainfall varies greatly across the island. The southern coast, which is usually the drier section of the island, averages 37 inches of rain (94 centimeters) per year. In the northern section of the island, rainfall is considerably heavier, averaging about 70 inches (180 centimeters) per year. With daily rain, is it any wonder that one of Puerto Rico's main tourist attractions is the Rain Forest? This forest, fertile and deep green, covers the El Yunque mountain and its nearby valleys. Here, the rainfall sometimes averages more than 200 inches (510 centimeters) per year.

Despite the rain, Puerto Rico's climate is close to ideal. Although it is more humid in the summer season, the average temperature in July is only 79 degrees Fahrenheit (26 degrees Centigrade), while in January it is 73 degrees F (22 degrees C). Constant sea breezes blowing across the island make the summer humidity much more bearable than it is on the United States mainland, and in Puerto Rico you will never find snow, frost, or even hail. Hurricanes, though, are another matter. From June through November, the island is on the alert for oncoming hurricanes, even though they occur only once every ten years or so. The National Weather Service can predict these storms hours or even days in advance, and storm alerts are published in the newspapers and announced on radio and television in an effort to prepare the people for the coming high winds and rain.

Puerto Rico's climate, considered its best natural resource, is an asset in the cultivation of crops. But climate cannot make up for the island's general lack of arable land. Although one third of its surface is suitable for agriculture, only 5 percent of the land is actually fertile. Because of the many streams and rivers, and because the island has more than 350 types of soil, soil erosion is a problem; the government tries to maintain land reserves for reforestation and erosion control. Another method of avoiding erosion is the contour planting of crops, designing fields to follow the natural contours (curves and ridges) of the land, where erosion is least likely to occur.

Gold could once be found on Puerto Rico; whatever small supply of it existed, however, was soon panned out. No coal exists

Farm workers dig an irrigation ditch in a field of plantains (a banana-like fruit that is a staple of the Caribbean diet); such ditches are contoured to prevent erosion

on the island, but the presence of oil is suspected. What Puerto Rico surely has, however, are natural minerals such as limestone, sand, gravel (mainly in San Juan and Ponce), and volcanic rock. The limestone is used to produce cement, while the sand is used in glass production. Water from the rivers is put to use in the manufacturing of hydro-generated power. Another source of electricity is thermal plants, which use imported fuels. There are several nickel and cobalt deposits on the island, as well as large deposits of valuable copper ore.

*Brilliant flowering
trees and plants
create a rainbow of
color in the
landscape*

Puerto Rico was once covered with forests; these are now gone, but the government has established 14 forest reserves that cover about 88,000 acres. If the island is lacking in forest area, it is not lacking in plant life: more than 3,000 types of plants grow in Puerto Rico. The blossoming trees are cherished for their beauty, particularly the *flamboyan* (poinciana) that sprouts blazing red flowers, the African tulip tree, and the mammoth *ceiba* (kapok) tree. Many of these trees bear fruits, such as breadfruit, star apples, sea grapes, papayas, and guanabanas, that cannot be found on the mainland. Both the poinsettia and the orchid are grown in Puerto Rico. Lining the coast are mangrove swamps (tropical trees with spreading branches that grow along the river) and coconut groves. These give way further inland to a combination of vegetation, notably the soft *yagruma* tree, which is similar to balsa wood. The dry southwestern region contains vegetation commonly found in a desert: bunchgrass and cacti.

18

Pineapples, bananas, and other tropical fruits flourish in the hot, moist climate; they are sold in every marketplace

Tobacco grown on the lower slopes of the mountains will be made into cigars in newly modernized factories

When we hear the word "tropical," we tend to think not only of vegetation but of wild—or at least rare—animals. On the island of Puerto Rico, however, there are none of the monkeys, alligators or large, wild mammals commonly associated with jungle life. During the evening hours you can hear the sweet song of the *coquí*, a small tree frog found only on the island. In addition to the coquí, many kinds of birds (including parrots), lizards, and harmless snakes inhabit the island. Insects too are associated with warm climates, and Puerto Rico has its share, from the *cucubano*, a tropical relative of the firefly, to mole crickets and termites. One unusual mammal found on the island is the Puerto Rico Fino Horse, which is admired for its delicate way of walking. Sea life consists of barracuda, herring, marlin, mullet, pompano, shark, snapper, Spanish mackerel, oysters, lobsters, and Puerto Rico's biggest catch, tuna.

20

The History of Puerto Rico

The Arawak Indians inhabited the island of Puerto Rico long before Christopher Columbus landed there on November 19, 1493. At the time of his arrival (during his second voyage to the New World), the island was called Boriquen or Borinquen, but Columbus renamed it San Juan Bautista (St. John the Baptist). Sent by Spain to take over the island, Ponce de Leon, who had served under Columbus, made his first settlement south of San Juan Bay at Caparra, which was renamed Ciudad de Puerto Rico (City of the Rich Port) in 1511.

The Arawaks did not want the Spanish to settle the island. They tried to fight the colonists, but de Leon and his troops quickly suppressed them. Within 75 years of de Leon's arrival, most of the Indians had fled the coastal regions and taken up residence in the mountains, where they married the whites and decided to take on Spanish ways.

In 1515, sugar cane was brought to Puerto Rico by way of Hispaniola in the West Indies, and three years later black slaves from Africa arrived. Since many of the Indians had died from disease or had been killed, the African blacks replaced them in the fields and in the mills. At the same time, Puerto Rico began to

21

A monument to Columbus, who landed on the island in 1493. Puerto Rico is the only place in the United States where he set foot

grow and export cotton, ginger, cacao, and indigo. By the early 17th century tobacco was being grown on the island, and by the 18th century the cultivation of coffee had begun.

Meanwhile, during the 16th century, Spain realized that its access to both the Caribbean Sea and the Atlantic Ocean put the colony of Puerto Rico in an excellent strategic location. The Spanish also recognized that Puerto Rico might have tremendous appeal to other European nations, and with this in mind began to secure the island—particularly the harbor at San Juan—by building fortresses to protect it against attack.

As the Spanish expected, in 1595 Puerto Rico was indeed attacked by Sir Francis Drake and Sir John Hawkins of England. In

22

1598, another British attack was waged against the island, this time by George Clifford, third Earl of Cumberland. This time, the English succeeded in capturing San Juan, but an outbreak of a deadly plague forced the attackers to leave the island within months. In 1625, the Dutch tried their hand at seizing the island, but their attempt failed after San Juan was burned in the struggle.

The English attacked once again in 1702. This time, they were successful in capturing Arecibo and within a year had landed at Loiza. Finally, in 1797, England tried once again to capture San Juan, but failed. This proved to be the last attack on Puerto Rico until the Spanish-American War.

Cannons at El Morro evoke Puerto Rico's embattled past

Until the outbreak of the Spanish-American War began to change the political status of Puerto Rico, the small population of the island had for three centuries been absolutely controlled by its mother country, Spain, and was permitted to trade only with Spain. During Spain's politically troubled years (roughly 1812 to 1836), the Spanish colonies were not granted many rights.

In 1868, a revolution broke out in Spain that affected Puerto Rico. A one-day skirmish called "El Grito de Lares" broke out in Puerto Rico, but the uprising was quickly beaten down. A year

An old etching shows the "Rich Port" in the early Spanish days

later, Spain finally listened to the cries of unrest on the island and proclaimed that Puerto Rico would become a province. By 1876, under the new Spanish constitution, discussions about whether or not Puerto Rico should remain under Spanish rule finally began. Cooperation between Luis Muñoz Rivera, leader of Puerto Rico's Autonomist Party, and Spanish Prime Minister Praxedes Mateo Sagasta resulted in a better understanding between Spain and the island. Puerto Rico was granted a so-called "independent" government, although its governor was still appointed by Spain.

Puerto Rico's new government did not last long, however. On April 21, 1898, the Spanish-American War began when American troops, under the control of Nelson A. Miles, landed at Guanicia. Unlike the first inhabitants of the island, who fought against the invaders, the Puerto Ricans looked to the United States as a source of hope for their future. The Treaty of Paris, signed on December 10, 1898, ended the Spanish-American War and gave Puerto Rico, Guam, and the Philippines to the United States. The U.S. Congress would now determine Puerto Rican rights.

When Puerto Rico became a temporary possession of the U.S., American currency and postage stamps were put into use on the island. On May 1, 1900, President William McKinley appointed Puerto Rico's first civil governor under the terms of the Foraker Act. The act called for: (1) duty-free (tax-free) trade between Puerto Rico and the United States and (2) exemption for Puerto Rico from contributing to the U.S. Treasury. Because of the Foraker Act, the sugar industry on the island began to boom, which in turn pulled the economy out of its slump.

During the 1920s and 1930s, however, the island again under-went hard times. The Depression of the 1930s battered Puerto Rico's economy, and two horrible hurricanes inflicted severe damage on the island. Despite economic hardships, the Puerto Rican population continued to grow, increasing from 953,000 in 1899 to 1,869,000 in 1940. This dramatic growth meant difficult years ahead for the crowded, economically depressed island. Help came by the late 1940s, in the form of an economic assistance program called "Operation Bootstrap," sponsored by the United States. Operation Bootstrap changed "the Poorhouse of the Caribbean" into an island with the highest per capita income in Latin America. Puerto Rico's net annual income per person rose from $121 in 1940 to more than $1,900 by the 1970s.

Puerto Rico has become a center of electronics manufacturing

In the harbor near Old San Juan, stone piers built by 15th-century Spanish settlers have recently been restored

In 1941, Puerto Rico's large farms were broken up and redistributed among farm workers. Education, which up to that time had not been a major concern, began to improve rapidly, reducing the illiteracy rate among Puerto Ricans. The slum dwellings that had covered the island were torn down to make way for more modern housing.

27

On July 25, 1946, President Harry S. Truman appointed Jesus Toribio Pinero the first native governor of Puerto Rico. One year later, the Puerto Rican government was granted permission to elect its own governor, and in 1948 it chose Luis Muñoz Marín, son of Luis Muñoz Rivera. The new governor believed that Puerto Rico should be a commonwealth linked to the United States. When the U.S. Congress passed Public Law 600 in 1950, it granted the island the power to write its own constitution. The Puerto Rican constitution was signed on July 1, 1952, and by July 25 of that year the tiny island had become a self-governing commonwealth.

By 1964, Governor Muñoz Marín decided to run for the Senate, so he persuaded his Popular Democratic Party to nominate Robert Sanchez Vilella as governor. Both Vilella and Muñoz Marín were elected. When Vilella ran for governor again in 1968, he organized a new party called the People's Party, but he lost the election to another important figure in Puerto Rican history, industrialist Luis Ferre, leader of the Progressive Party.

In the election of 1972, the Popular Party returned to power when Rafael Hernandez Colón was elected governor. One of Colón's first decisions was to form a statehood advisory committee, of which he made Muñoz Marín chairman. Back in the States, President Richard M. Nixon appointed Senator Marlow Cook joint chairman of the committee. In December 1975, the U.S. House of Representatives considered the committee's "Bill To Approve The Compact of Permanent Union Between Puerto Rico and the United States." The bill called for the replacement of the term "commonwealth" with the term "Free Associated State."

During the 1970s, Puerto Rico was again threatened by economic hardship. As the cost of fuels, raw materials and consumer products imported to the island increased, and as the recession in the United States reached its peak, Puerto Rico too felt the economic pinch, and high inflation countered the gains made earlier. In response to these problems, the government created new taxes, continued to promote industry, and lowered its spending budget. In the later 1970s, Puerto Rico began to recover from its setbacks. Increased tourism helped bring much-needed income to the island.

In the 1980 race for governor, Romero Barcelo, who campaigned to make Puerto Rico the 51st state of the United States, defeated Hernandez Colón. In the 1984 election, however, Barcelo lost to Colón, and the pro-commonwealth party again took power.

Many Caribbean cruise ships call at Puerto Rico

A National Park Service guide explains the features of one of the island's fortresses to schoolchildren on a tour of Old San Juan

The Puerto Rican People

Due to their Spanish origins and their proximity to the United States, the Puerto Rican people have a special heritage—a rare combination of the Old and New Worlds.

Puerto Rican people, like their Spanish ancestors, tend to be passionate. They are extremely expressive in their emotions—sensitive, sympathetic, and resentful of slights to them. They are hospitable and eager to open their homes to friends and newcomers. Their friendly nature also makes them fond of their *fiestas*, or holiday celebrations. But their most outstanding characteristic is their deep attachment to family life. The Puerto Rican family structure is a tight one. Puerto Rican youngsters and young adults cherish the love and approval of their parents. Because of the close family structure, children are reluctant to do anything that would harm their family's reputation. As long as children remain under their parents' roof, they adhere to their parents' rules. This allegiance to kin extends well beyond the immediate family; respect for grandparents, aunts, uncles, and even distant relatives is a way of life for the Puerto Rican people. The family has evolved as a type of support system on the island; in times of great stress in Puerto Rico's history, family life has helped to unify the people. Of course, the changes in the American family unit have affected Puerto Rico in recent years, and Puerto Rican values have changed slightly. Nevertheless, the home continues to be a place of comfort, warmth, and family solidarity.

Intermarriage between Puerto Rico's original Indian, white, and black inhabitants has made Puerto Rican society a mixture of three races. As in many societies, different racial groups have congregated in different areas of the country. For example, the black heritage is more prominent on the coasts, and the mountains still contain many people of Indian extraction, descendants of those Indians who fled to the mountains after the arrival of the Spanish.

The class structure of the island differs slightly from that of the American mainland. The United States has distinct upper, middle, and lower classes. In Puerto Rico, there are only two classes: a very small upper class (almost entirely Spanish) and a large lower class. Within the last few decades, however, changes in the island's economy and growing economic ties to the outside world have led to the emergence of a middle class.

Although several Protestant missionary groups are active on the island, Puerto Rico is, like Spain, a Roman Catholic state. Four out of every five Puerto Ricans are Catholic; members of the Assemblies of God, Baptist, Methodist, and Presbyterian churches make up the non-Catholic population. The Puerto Rican constitution provides for the separation of church and state, just as the United States constitution does; still, Roman Catholic customs and rituals—particularly the celebration of feast days and Catholic holidays—are an important part of daily Puerto Rican life.

This statue commemorates brave women who prevented a British attack by marching through San Juan carrying torches; the British retreated, believing that Spanish reinforcements had arrived

The ornate altar of the Catedral de San Juan

34

Puerto Rico is a densely populated island; in the mainland United States, only New Jersey has more people living in one area. Of the 3,196,520 people living on the island, more than half live in the metropolitan areas of Caguas, Ponce, Mayaguez, and San Juan. The country people of Puerto Rico live in small houses, not only because of low income but because they spend so much time out of doors. When they are not meeting at each other's homes, the country people gather at the *colmado*, the village general store. The colmado is thought of as a community center, where the people of each village can talk with each other and enjoy each other's company.

Puerto Rican food is, of course, a blend of influences. The great variety of sea life from the surrounding waters make fish, particularly tuna, a common dish. Spanish food—dishes like *paella* (a rice and seafood mixture) and *gazpacho* (a cold soup)— is also enjoyed on the island. The hotels feature various types of food, from Spanish gourmet dishes featuring lamb and rice to the best French foods. And all kinds of American food, from the finest fare to common hamburgers and french fries, are available on the island.

Culture and Celebration

Although the establishment of commonwealth status in Puerto Rico was of great political importance, independence for the island had far-reaching cultural effects as well. Commonwealth status permitted the people to develop their own identity through music, the creative and visual arts, literature, and island celebrations. Let's examine some of the cultural traditions and annual events of this island.

Because the Puerto Ricans are a passionate and festive people who take their religious life seriously, one of the most striking features of life on the island is the frequent observation of what are known in the Catholic religion as feast days. Each town has its own patron saint, and it is not unusual to find carnival celebrations taking place for several days at the time of the saint's feast day. These celebrations feature dancing, singing, gambling (which is legal on the island), amusement park rides, and many processions and religious ceremonies. One of the biggest celebrations takes place in San Juan. It includes the crowning of the "Carnival Queen," who remains the island's "Queen of Queens" for a year. The ritual of electing a queen is based on the Catholic devotion to the Virgin Mary or Blessed Mother, and it is taken very seriously

Carnival performers line the streets during festivals, which usually include several days of singing, dancing, gambling, and parades

by the young girls (usually chosen from the upper classes) who participate. Boys and men in Puerto Rico enjoy watching the Latin American sport of cockfighting, which is held on the weekends in *galleras*, or cock pits.

Puerto Rico's list of annual events is extensive. A number of holidays are celebrated on the island—many of them religious—

37

that do not occur on the mainland. For instance, King's Day, celebrated on January 6th of each year, marks the official end of the Christmas season. Not only do children receive gifts on Christmas Day, but they receive gifts on King's Day as well. Between January and June, some of the holidays and celebrations include: the birthday of Puerto Rican essayist Eugenio Maria de Hostos; the Ponce de Leon Carnival, held in San Juan in mid-February; the Dulce Sueno Paso Fino Horse Show, held in Guayama in late February; the Miss Puerto Rico Pageant in early May; the Puerto Rican Theatre Festival in Old San Juan; and the Eve of San Juan Bautista Day on June 23rd.

Between July and December, Puerto Ricans celebrate: Constitution Day, which marks the adoption of the Puerto Rican constitution in 1952; the *Dia de la Raza*, the "Day of the Race" or Columbus Day, on October 12th; and Discovery Day, which marks Columbus's arrival in Puerto Rico, celebrated on November 19th. The lively Puerto Ricans know how to make their day-to-day existence a joyful one.

In addition to these festivals, carnivals, feast days, and political holidays, the Puerto Ricans have a rich cultural life. The Institute of Puerto Rican Culture, established by the government in 1955, designs programs in archeology, music, architecture, literature, drama, and dance. At the same time, the Department of Parks and Recreation on the island has developed parks and baseball fields, and has offered Spanish-language plays and courses in dramatics, folk dancing, and native music. Mobile theatrical companies and bookmobiles often tour the island.

This santos is called "Tres Reyes Magos" ("Three Magi Kings")

Although handicrafts—the making of pottery, baskets, and other artifacts—are not extensively practiced on the island, Puerto Rico does have a famous art form: the *santos*. The santos are small wooden saints, Virgins, and Magi carved by a diminishing group of artisans known as the *santeros*. These carved objects can still

Pablo Casals, one of the world's greatest cellists, was proud of his Puerto Rican heritage and settled on the island

occasionally be purchased in gift shops on the island, although very few of them are produced today.

People who love celebration are also people who love music, which forms a large part of any celebration in Puerto Rico. The two most famous forms of music are the *decima*, which is the music of the hill people, and the *plena*, the folk music of the coastal blacks. The decima is a rhyming contest in which each of the contestants makes up verses about a person or event on the island; the verses are then set to music. The plena is similar to the Latin American calypso (commonly referred to as the cha-cha) and also deals with current island subjects.

In addition to the folk music of the people, Puerto Rico has more formal music. Puerto Rico's greatest composer was Juan Morell Campos (1857–1898), whose music is still popular today. Another well-known Puerto Rican composer was Rafael Hernandez (1889–1965) whose music is known throughout Latin America. But the greatest boost to the musical heritage of Puerto Rico was the arrival of the world-famous Spanish cellist, Pablo Casals, who came to San Juan in 1956. Casals, whose mother was Puerto Rican, eventually made his home on the island, and the annual Casals Festival attracts not only the islanders but an international audience as well. Under Casals's direction, Puerto Rico established a first-rate symphony orchestra. Initially, musicians for the orchestra had to be brought in from other nations, but with the establishment of the Conservatory of Music in 1959, native Puerto Ricans could study and train under a distinguished faculty that included noted pianist Jesus Maria Sanroma.

The literature of Puerto Rico, like that of many Latin American countries, often refers to social and political issues. Most of Puerto Rico's important literature was produced in the late 19th century. Among the island's most noted authors are Manuel A. Alonso, who recreated the voice of the *jibaro* (peasant) in his poetry and prose, and Alejandro Tapia, whose literary talents took many forms, including an allegorical poem, a play called *The Quadroon Woman*, and a volume of memoirs dealing with life in mid-19th-century San Juan.

Silkscreen prints by Luis G. Cajiga depict island life: men playing dominoes and a bright street scene

New writing styles and new waves of thought came to Puerto Rico in the 20th century. Luis Llorens Torres was the first major 20th-century Puerto Rican poet. After Torres came a group of intellectuals known as the "Generation of the Thirties," whose works, aimed at defining the true Puerto Rican identity, include *Insularism*, by Antonio Padriera, and *The Historical Summary of Puerto Rico*, by Tomas Blanco.

In the years following World War II, Puerto Rican literature continued to develop. A number of plays by Puerto Rican authors have contributed to the growth of the island's theater, and writers of novels and stories have explored the subject of the Puerto Rican experience in New York. It is clear that Puerto Rico has a diverse and ever-changing culture to share with the world.

Transportation and Communication

The island of Puerto Rico has about 7,700 miles (12,392 kilometers) of surfaced roads. The most common means of transportation on the island is automobiles, followed by buses, trucks, and cabs. In 1975, 774,000 vehicles were registered, more than four

Luxury liners dock in San Juan's harbor, a major port for cargo and passenger ships

times the number registered in 1960. And since 1975, that number has almost doubled. The reason for so many motor vehicles on the island is that, despite industry and manufacturing, Puerto Rico has no railroad system. The uneven surface of the island—from marshy lowlands to mountainous regions—probably accounts for the absence of railroads.

Puerto Rico's dependence on ocean shipping led the government to purchase its own merchant fleet in 1974. The Puerto Rican Maritime Authority presides over the merchant fleet, and vessels travel easily between the island and the mainland ports. Both American and foreign shipping companies provide transpor-

tation service for cargo, but all passenger travel to the island is by air. Puerto Rico's three chief seaports are San Juan in the north, Mayaguez in the west, and Ponce in the south.

Puerto Rico International Airport, called San Juan International Airport when it opened in 1955, is the island's largest airport. It serves more than five million passengers each year, and 20 different airlines land on its runways. In addition to Puerto Rico International, the island has at least six smaller airports. Ponce's airport has recently been enlarged to handle planes from the United States. All the ports in Puerto Rico, whether air or sea, are governed by the Ports Authority, an agency that functions under Puerto Rico's rule and has no connection to the Ports Authority in the United States.

For a long time, the Puerto Rican government both owned and operated the telegraph service, but in 1974 it purchased the

Tankers unload at a new 66,000-barrel-a-day refinery in Yabucda

Planes from around the world land at Puerto Rico International Airport

I.T.T. corporation's telephone installations on the island. These are now operated by the government's Telephone Authority.

Puerto Rico's first radio station, WKAQ, began broadcasting from San Juan in 1922. At that time, all broadcasts were in Spanish. In 1954, WKAQ built Puerto Rico's first television station, also in San Juan. The first television shows carried by WKAQ were made in Puerto Rico, but now Puerto Ricans can tune in to shows from the mainland United States. Today, there are about 90 radio stations and about 10 television stations on the island. In addition to commercial stations, the Department of Education runs both a radio and a television station, dedicated exclusively to shows dealing with cultural or educational matters.

47

Another means of communication on the island is newspapers. The first newspaper was *El Dia (The Day),* founded in Ponce in 1909. Now the most important Spanish newspapers published on the island are *El Mundo (The World), El Nuevo Dia (The New Day),* and *El Vocero (The Voice).* The English-language newspaper is the San Juan *Star. The Star* is a production of the Scripps-Howard Enterprise, which publishes many newspapers in the United States. The hotels sell many of the magazines found on the mainland, some of them available in Spanish or English.

It may seem strange to think of a Caribbean island as having all the comforts of a large, highly mechanized society. But Puerto Rico manages to offer a quiet retreat from the world while remaining a vital part of it.

Many Puerto Ricans today work in the electronics industry; here, computer parts are assembled in San German, a small city in the southwestern part of the island

Government

One question Puerto Rico has had to ask repeatedly over the centuries is "Who's in charge?" The island has had many forms of government. Once a colony under Spanish rule, Puerto Rico has also been, under United States authority, a possession, a commonwealth, and—at least in name—an "associated free state." In fact, Puerto Rico is still a commonwealth and will maintain that status as long as the pro-commonwealth party stays in office. Because government hierarchies can sometimes be confusing, let's look carefully at the present Puerto Rican governing body.

There are two documents on which Puerto Rico's leaders base the decisions that govern the people. These two documents, enacted in 1952, are the Constitution of the Commonwealth of Puerto Rico and the Federal Relations Statute. The constitution defines the terms and procedures of Puerto Rico's internal government, and the laws of the constitution pertain only to Puerto Rico, not to the American mainland. Nevertheless, these internal rules are similar to the way the government in the U.S. works.

Just as we do in the United States, Puerto Ricans elect a two-chamber legislature, which has the power and responsibility to make laws. The executive branch is made up of the highest governing officials, and the judicial branch serves the courts.

The Federal Relations Statute defines relations between Puerto Rico and the U.S. federal government. Under the terms of this statute, the federal government handles all foreign relations and defense for Puerto Rico, and manages the island's postal system, customs service, agricultural experiment station, and soil erosion service. The statute defines Puerto Ricans as citizens of the United States, but they do not have the right to vote for president. Puerto Rico has a resident commissioner in the U.S. House of Representatives who has a say in all legislation that affects Puerto Rico but cannot vote on bills before the House. Although

The home of the Puerto Rico Federal Affairs Administration

Old-style Spanish architecture has been restored

the commonwealth is eligible for aid in the form of grants, just as any U.S. state is, Puerto Ricans do not pay federal taxes. The men of Puerto Rico are subject to the military draft.

All Puerto Rican citizens have the right to vote in Puerto Rican elections at age 18. To be a citizen of Puerto Rico, a person must either be born there or be a citizen of the United States who has lived for at least one year on the island.

Every four years, Puerto Ricans vote to elect their legislature, on the same day as the presidential election in the United States— the Tuesday after the first Monday in November. Members of the Puerto Rican House of Representatives and the Senate are elected, usually 51 representatives and 27 senators. Two of the senators are chosen from each of the senatorial districts, while 11 are designated at large. As for the representatives, one is elected from each of the 40 districts and another 11 are representatives at large. At least one-third of the seats in the legislature must be filled by minority parties, to ensure that all voices are being heard and represented in the government. Whenever one party wins more than two-thirds of the legislative seats, the legislature is enlarged to provide for the one-third representation of the opposite parties.

The executive branch of the government is headed by the governor, who is elected by direct vote in a general election. Just like the president in the United States, the governor is inaugurated on January 2nd and holds office for four years. He appoints members of his cabinet with the consent and counsel of the commonwealth Senate. To appoint a secretary of state, the governor also needs the consent of the House of Representatives. The secretary

53

of state also serves as the lieutenant governor, who acts as governor whenever the actual governor is absent from the island or if the governor dies or is removed from office.

The executive branch has 14 departments: Justice, State, Education, Treasury, Labor, Public Health, Agriculture, Commerce, Transportation and Public Works, Social Services, Consumer Affairs, Housing, Addiction Services, and Natural Resources. The governor appoints all of the secretaries who head these departments, as well as the heads of a number of government corporations and administrations. All of these appointees have cabinet status. Another part of the executive branch is the Planning Board, which coordinates the works of the various departments and is attached directly to the office of the governor.

Puerto Rico's flag has the same colors as the United States flag

At La Fortaleza, the governor's mansion near San Juan Harbor, the flags of Puerto Rico and the United States fly side by side

As in the United States, the highest court in Puerto Rico is the Supreme Court, made up of a chief justice and eight associate justices. Each justice is appointed by the governor with the advice and consent of the Senate and the House. The justices hold office "during good behavior," which means that their terms are for an indefinite number of years. Judges in the lower courts are also appointed by the governor, but they have definite terms of office. Judges of the federal court district for Puerto Rico are chosen by the president of the United States.

Although the United States is responsible for the handling of all foreign relations for Puerto Rico, the commonwealth government, through its Department of State, works very closely with

A walk through Old San Juan is a walk into Puerto Rico's past

the United States in educational or cultural issues.

The local government in Puerto Rico is markedly different from local governments in the United States. Puerto Rico has no counties; the basic unit of local government is the *municipio* (municipality). There are 78 municipalities in Puerto Rico and the voters in each of these elect a mayor and an assembly. In turn, the mayor appoints a secretary and a treasurer. The cities, towns, and villages of the municipalities do not choose their own governing bodies, but are instead governed by the appointed officials of the municipality.

Puerto Rico has two major political parties: the Popular Democratic Party, which wants Puerto Rico to keep its commonwealth

status, and the New Progressive Party, which is in favor of statehood. The question of statehood is hotly debated in Puerto Rico today, with most of the islanders holding strong views on one side or the other of the issue.

Other political parties in Puerto Rico are the Independence Party and the Renovation Party. Political parties that receive at least 5 percent of the votes in Puerto Rican elections receive financial support from a fund provided by the government.

The major sources of revenue for the government are income and excise taxes and federal grants and aid. The Puerto Rican government spends about 50 percent of its budget on education, health, and welfare. By 1975, government expenditures had reached $1.8 billion, mainly due to the government's purchase of the telephone company and its loans to the Sugar Corporation. Each year tourists pour approximately $424 million into Puerto Rico. The governor's salary, while comfortable, is a modest $35,000 per year—about as much as a middle-management executive in the United States. The governor lives in the official governor's mansion in San Juan. The mansion is actually the old fortress of La Fortaleza, which looks out onto San Juan Bay. In front of La Fortaleza, the flags of Puerto Rico and the United States fly side by side.

Graceful La Fortaleza, now the governor's mansion, was built as a fortress in the 1500s

Schools and Universities

At one time, most Puerto Ricans could not read or write, and the government did not consider education a high priority. Over the years, however, education has become increasingly important on the island. In 1950, total enrollment in the public school system—both elementary and secondary schools—was 410,000; by the mid-1970s, it had increased to more than 700,000. Today, the commonwealth has about 31,000 teachers for more than 800,000 students.

Although Spanish is spoken in the schools, all students are required to learn English. In fact, some schools teach English as early as the first grade. The public school system includes vocational schools, which train some 180,000 students (including 35,000 adults) in the skills necessary to work in industry. The Division of Community Education, which oversees vocational training, also directs programs to educate Puerto Rico's rural poor. Another government agency, the Department of Education, is responsible for adult education programs designed to eliminate illiteracy in Puerto Rico.

Puerto Rico has 13 colleges and universities, all accredited by the Middle States Association of Colleges and Schools, just as

A clock tower looms above the University of Puerto Rico's San Juan campus

schools and colleges are accredited in the United States. Perhaps the best known of these institutions is the University of Puerto Rico, founded in 1903. It is coeducational and government-controlled, with campuses in Rio Piedras, Mayaguez, and San Juan. The main campus, located at Rio Piedras, includes colleges of the humanities, natural sciences, social sciences, business administration, education, pharmacy, law, architecture, general studies, and the Graduate School of Librarianship.

61

Puerto Rican schoolchildren gather around their teacher during a botanical field trip to the rain forest

Colleges of arts and sciences, agricultural sciences, and business administration, as well as the School of Education, are located at the University's Mayaguez campus. The San Juan campus contains the schools of dentistry, medicine, audiology, physical and occupational therapy, and speech pathology.

More than 50,000 students attend the University of Puerto Rico, where they receive degrees such as the bachelor of arts in law, science, and business; the bachelor of science in nursing, pharmacy, and physical therapy; the master of arts in public

The powerful radio telescope at Arecibo helps scientists explore the frontiers of space

administration, public health, science, and social work; and the doctor of dental medicine, medicine, and philosophy. The colleges at Humaco, Cayey, Ponce, Bayamon, Agudilla, Arecibo, and Carolina are all affiliated with the University of Puerto Rico.

In the hills south of Arecibo, a giant radio telescope has been erected to study outer space. Heavy cables support the telescope's 500-foot (165-meter) antenna, and the reflector measures 1,000 feet (330 meters) in diameter.

The recent emphasis on education has also led to the development of libraries. Each of the island's universities maintains an excellent library, and the Department of Education sends bookmobiles all over Puerto Rico from its large library in San Juan. The Ateneo de Puerto Rico, a cultural society, has a library of Puerto Rican culture in San Juan, and the Teacher's Association and the Lions Club each maintain a library. The privately supported Volunteer Library League of San Juan has built a bilingual library for both Spanish and English speakers.

How the Puerto Ricans Make Their Living

In the 1960s, Puerto Rico became a haven for refugees from other Latin American countries. After Fidel Castro came to power in Cuba, Puerto Rico opened its shores to over 20,000 Cuban refugees, who were soon followed by thousands of people fleeing unrest in the Dominican Republic. The 1980 census reported that Puerto Rico's population had swelled to more than three million people, an average of 2,780 people per square mile. As a result of this dramatic increase, Puerto Rico faced the problem of providing jobs for the thousands of people in need of income. Efforts have been made to diversify manufacturing and industry to meet the need for jobs.

Modern equipment is used to harvest sugar cane,
one of Puerto Rico's most important crops

Many Puerto Rican women have recently entered the workforce with jobs in the garment industry, the island's leading employer

The leading employer in Puerto Rico is the clothing industry; more than 36,000 people work making garments and footwear. Many of them are women who have recently entered the workforce after years as wives and mothers. The food service industry is the island's second largest employer, with more than 20,000 workers processing sugar, rum, cigars and other tobacco products, flour, and rice. New industrial plants produce paper products, furniture, metal cans, rubber, plastics, scientific instruments, and various types of heavy machinery. Other industries in Puerto Rico make electronic equipment and pharmaceuticals. In all, some 202,000 workers are employed in the island's 2,400 factories. In Ponce, oil refineries provide jobs for many Puerto Ricans; the refineries are the principal reason why Puerto Rico has the highest standard of living in the Caribbean.

Another source of employment in Puerto Rico is agriculture, which each year yields $547 million in goods—10 percent of the value of all goods produced on the island. Puerto Rico's farms provide many of the raw materials for the large food service industry. Sugar cane, coffee, and tobacco are leading crops.

Much of the island's sugar cane production is managed jointly by the Land Authority, an arm of the government, and the Sugar Corporation, which was established in 1973. Modern methods of sugar manufacturing are now used—cane that was once harvested by field hands with machetes is now cut by machine, and old sugar mills have been updated with modern equipment. Although wages in the sugar industry have steadily increased, many sugar

Oil refineries at Ponce have greatly aided the economy

The coastal valleys are the island's most productive farming region; here, cattle graze under palm trees on a dairy farm

workers have abandoned the mills to take jobs in the large cloth-ing and chemical industries.

Puerto Rico's coffee industry also employs many people. Originally, the lack of shade trees on the island made it difficult to grow coffee, but now a new type of coffee that does not require shade is being planted. Employment in the tobacco industry has also increased recently, as cigar factories have been improved with modern machinery.

Many Puerto Ricans who do not work in the manufacturing or agricultural fields are employed in the fishing industry, which produces an annual catch valued at $102 million, or in the mining industry, which yields an annual income of $134 million. Some also find employment in the electric power plants.

Imports and Exports

All trade between the United States and Puerto Rico is similar to trade between states on the mainland. When Puerto Rico trades with the United States, it does not have to pay the customs duties it would be required to pay on goods imported from other places.

The Condado Strip is famous for its miles of marble-white beaches

Of the nearly $5 billion in goods Puerto Rico imports each year, 60 percent comes from the United States, mostly raw materials for industry and consumer goods. Puerto Rico also imports crude oil from Venezuela.

Long ago, the most important items Puerto Rico exported to the United States were molasses, rum, and sugar. These are still exported in large quantities, but today, Puerto Rico's most valuable exports are chemicals, food products, machinery, tobacco products, textiles, petroleum products, and toys. The city of Mayaguez has a foreign trade zone where manufacturers can display, process, and reship their products without paying customs duties.

Many of these pineapples will be exported to the mainland

The economy depends heavily on exports, including toys made in new factories like this one

The Tourist Trade

A new but important source of jobs and income for Puerto Rico is tourism—one of the biggest elements of the island's economy. Waiters, chefs, tour guides, casino employees, bartenders, hotel managers, and others support the tourism industry, which is busiest from November through April.

Most tourism jobs can be found in San Juan, although Mayaguez, Ponce, Arecibo, and the islands of Culebra and Vieques receive visitors also. Several completely self-contained resort areas are dotted around the coastline, in out-of-the-way places like Dorado Beach and Palmas del Mar; they provide employment for local villagers. In addition, the government maintains a number of *paradores*, or guest houses, in the interior of the island—one paradore popular with tourists is Gripiñas, in the hills above Ponce, which was made from a 19th-century coffee plantation.

Puerto Rican officials believe that tourism will increase. The tourist trade, in fact, is expected to become the economic mainstay of the island, although industrial and commercial development will continue as well.

La Mina waterfall is a breathtaking sight in the Caribbean National Forest on El Yunque Mountain

Touring the Island

Tourists and travelers have found that Puerto Rico offers a great variety of activities and sights, from the "Americanized" cafes, discos, and restaurants of the island's many hotels to the churches, forts, and other landmarks dating from the Spanish years. Because tourism is such big business for Puerto Rico, the government publishes a monthly magazine called *Que Pasa (What's Happening)*, which gives visitors detailed descriptions of events and attractions on the island.

Although tourists come to Puerto Rico for every type of vacation—from sunbathing on a palm-fringed beach to rubbing elbows with the international jet set in the casinos—most visits to the island begin in San Juan. The capital city is a mix of the past and the present. Old colonial fortresses, now moss-covered and serene, share the skyline with dazzling new glass-and-steel skyscrapers.

Old San Juan, founded in 1521, has been completely restored; architects have tried to preserve or recreate the original colonial style with whitewashed walls, black wrought-iron balconies, and narrow, winding cobblestone streets. Today Old San Juan is one of the island's biggest tourist attractions. It is dominated by El Morro fortress, which covers more than 200 acres and rises to a height of 145 feet (44 meters) above the sea on the very tip of the peninsula where San Juan stands. The Park Service maintains El Morro and conducts daily tours; visitors especially enjoy the labyrinth of tunnels that lies beneath the fort. From the ramparts, you can look down over the old Spanish cemetery, which contains an unusual circular chapel.

Near El Morro is San José Church, one of the oldest sites of Christian worship in the New World. Ponce de Leon, the island's first governor, was buried in San Jose. His body remained there for three-and-a-half centuries until it was transferred to the city's big cathedral, and his coat of arms still hangs from the ceiling. A

Fort San Cristobal sits on the outskirts of contemporary San Juan

nearby convent, Santo Domingo, was built in the 16th century, served as an army headquarters during the 19th century, and now houses the Institute of Puerto Rican Culture, a museum of island art. The Institute includes a library of 16th- and 17th-century books and a patio where German-style tuba bands play on Friday nights.

This ancient ball park was built by the Taino Indians, a tribe of the Arawak people

The San Juan harbor, one of the world's great natural harbors, has been enlarged and modernized as part of a multi-million-dollar restoration program. Old stone piers were repaired and new concrete ones built. Near the piers is the Crafts Plaza, with a restaurant and a number of shops selling souvenirs, ceramics, and beachwear. The harbor and the Crafts Plaza were designed to attract tourists and to obtain business from the passengers of the Caribbean cruise ships that call at San Juan.

Colonial Houses

Among the old houses now open to the public in Old San Juan are: La Casa del Libro, which houses a world-famous museum of rare books; Casa Blanca, begun in 1521 to be the residence of Ponce de Leon (he died looking for the Fountain of Youth in Florida before he could move in); and Casa de los Contrafuertes, or House of Buttresses, which contains a priceless collection of carved santos.

New San Juan appeals to tourists, too. The luxury hotels on the Condado Strip beachfront, the reef at Boca de Cangrejos near

The Taino, the island's original inhabitants, created these mysterious rock carvings, called petroglyphs

the airport (a favorite with snorkelers and scuba divers), and the Botanical Gardens in the southern suburb of Rio Piedras (where you can walk through a bamboo forest and a huge orchid garden) are three sources of revenue for Puerto Rico. Gamblers enjoy El Commandante racetrack and the blackjack and roulette tables in the hotels. Tourists interested in sea life can visit the Ocean Life Park Aquarium, home of many tropical fish, sea lions, and dolphins.

One of the most exciting ways to see Puerto Rico is to drive the length of the Ruta Panoramica, or Scenic Highway, which runs

Boats cross the harbor beyond El Morro's battlements

Sports like windsurfing attract thousands of tourists to the island each year

along the crest of the Cordillera Central mountain range from San Juan to Ponce and offers spectacular views. Cabo Rojo, a small town on the dry southwestern coast (called "desert" by the Puerto Ricans), was once the hideout of the pirate Roberto Cofresi. Nearby San German was founded in 1573 and boasts Porta Coeli (Gate of Heaven) Church, built in 1606—the oldest intact church in the United States or its dependencies. Camuy, west of Arecibo on the northern coast, is the site of many caves,

After only six months, the plantains are taller than the farmer

which geologists and spelunkers enjoy exploring. Mayaguez, on the western coast, is Puerto Rico's needlework headquarters; it's a good place to buy fine embroidery. A zoo and an institute of tropical agriculture are also located in Mayaguez, the island's third largest city.

Ponce, on the southern coast, is sometimes called "the Pearl of the South." Although it is not well known to tourists, Ponce is Puerto Rico's second largest city and hopes to become an important tourist center. It offers a cathedral, many colonial buildings, beaches and outdoor markets, and a bright red and black firehouse with vivid yellow fire engines (much photographed by visitors).

El Yunque Rain Forest

One of the most popular destinations with tourists is El Yunque, a rain forest that covers 28,000 acres on the slopes of El Yunque Mountain, about an hour's drive from San Juan. Nearly 100 billion gallons of rain fall here each year, and the area is thick with lush vegetation—more than 240 species of trees and many kinds of tropical flowers. Close to El Yunque, on the coast, is Luqillo Beach, one of the largest beaches of the Caribbean, with white sand and clear water. Once a coconut plantation, Luqillo is now open to the public.

Other attractions include: the ancient Taino Indian "ball park"; La Parguera, a resort noted for fishing; and the famous Phosphorescent Bay, so named because on moonless nights it shimmers with the large number of plankton (microscopic animals and plants) that flash light into the water.

Parador Gripiñas (above) is a popular guest house in a former coffee plantation; the round towers of El Morro (right) are Puerto Rico's most distinctive architectural feature

82

Vieques and Culebra

Vieques and Culebra, two small islands off Puerto Rico's eastern coast, recently have become tourist attractions. Culebra is noted for its beaches and coral reefs; Vieques also has several beaches and a newly discovered phosphorescent bay, even brighter than the famous one on Puerto Rico's southern coast, that may become an important source of revenue. Both islands can be reached by ferry. And just a short boat ride away from Puerto Rico is the

Puerto Rico's serene natural beauty is an economic asset

***Tourists enjoy sights like the Park of the Doves in Old San Juan; they
bring welcome revenue to the island***

island of St. Thomas in the United States Virgin Islands. Known for
its pale pastel houses and narrow cobblestone streets, St. Thomas
is a good place for shoppers to find bargains on liquor, jewelry,
and clothing. Many visitors to Puerto Rico make day-trips to St.
Thomas in boats operated by Puerto Ricans.

The money spent by tourists in Puerto Rico—not only in San
Juan but in villages and small towns around the coast and throughout the interior—is a significant part of the island's total income.
Government planners hope that tourism will continue to increase
and to play a major role in Puerto Rico's economy. For this reason,
the island's natural beauty and colonial heritage are being preserved carefully.

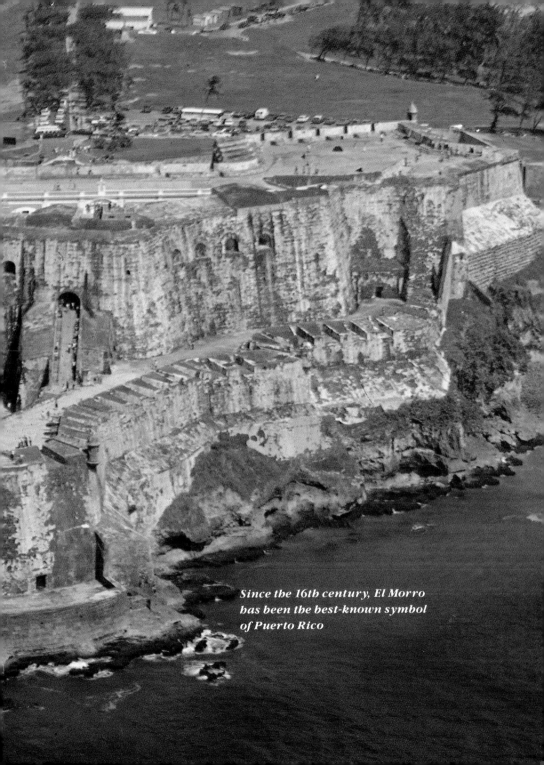

Since the 16th century, El Morro has been the best-known symbol of Puerto Rico

Puerto Rico's Place in the World

The names of Puerto Rico's newspapers show that the island, once inhabited only by Indians and little known to the rest of the world, has now gained international importance. The island's first newspaper, called *El Dia (The Day),* concerned itself with matters of interest only to islanders. Now, however, *El Mundo (The World)* reflects Puerto Rico's interest in world affairs.

No longer is Puerto Rico a backward island, cut off from other nations by language or cultural barriers. It has evolved into a bilingual and—more important—a bicultural commonwealth, able to retain its rich Spanish heritage but not afraid to incorporate Anglo-American influences as well.

As education continues to grow on the island, so will the number of professional people. The number of dentists, nurses, doctors, professors, and scientists will grow, expanding what has been a society composed mostly of farm and factory workers. Those Puerto Ricans who have come to America's urban areas have acquired skills and ideas that they can take back to their homeland to make it an even better place for its three million-plus inhabitants. Those who remain on the mainland bring with them a heritage that can enrich the lives of the people in the United States.

88

Puerto Rico has created for itself a unique place in the world by moving forward in industry and trade while preserving many details of its rich Spanish heritage

89

The Catedral de San Juan contains a shrine to St. Pius

Certainly, the open and festive nature of the Puerto Rican people is a characteristic any nation would welcome and learn from.

Puerto Ricans have every reason to be proud of their fellow islanders who have gained success in a variety of fields. Puerto Rico has enriched the film industry on the mainland and throughout the world with actors like Jose Ferrer. Actress Rita Moreno starred in the classic movie *West Side Story*. Jose Feliciano, noted for his hit "Light My Fire," is known and respected around the

world as a singer and guitarist. The sports world will never forget Roberto Clemente, an outfielder for the Pittsburgh Pirates baseball team. He died in an airplane crash as he was flying to Puerto Rico to aid the victims of a terrible hurricane. It was Clemente's strong sense of duty and allegiance to his people that inspired him to go to Puerto Rico to help the victims of the storm. And, of course, the great Pablo Casals will always be remembered for his influence on the world of music.

If Columbus and Ponce de Leon could see Puerto Rico today, they would surely be astonished at the sight of a Sheraton or Hilton hotel on an island that was mostly forest and lush plant life when they first saw it centuries ago. They would be confused and frightened by the cars, the airports, the factories, the universities, and the mills. One look at La Fortaleza or at the rooftop in the plaza at Ponce, however, and they would know that although many things in Puerto Rico have changed and developed, the old is still very much bound up with the new. Although Puerto Rico is an island of everyday things—hotels, tourism, hamburgers, television—it is also an island of the rare and exotic. Only in Puerto Rico can you hear the *coqui* singing in the Caribbean night.

The late baseball star Roberto Clemente is an island hero

Index

93

X 5/02-2 Ages 8-12   TI5275
8/04-2
9/10/13=2   10/10/15=3
10/22/14=3   8/25/20-3(14)

Williston Park Public Library

494 Willis Avenue

Williston Park, New York

WP